The Art of Lutherie

by Tom Bills

Online Video

Video
dv.melbay.com/30105

You Tube
www.melbay.com/30105V

THEARTOFLUTHERIE.COM

1 2

Visit us on the Web at www.melbay.com — E-mail us at email@melbay.com

Foreword

I first learned of Tom Bills Custom Guitars at the inaugural (now-defunct) Great Midwest Guitar Show in St. Louis, Missouri. I was a high schooler hellbent on becoming a hardcore jazz guitarist. By that time in my life I had easily put in 10,000 hours of practice on guitar—I had as good a feel for what made a decent instrument as perhaps anyone my age. I had also played signature guitars crafted by some of the most renowned luthiers in history: D'Angelico (I played several, including Mel Bay's Mel Bay New Yorker and a non-cutaway of his); D'Aquisto (again, I played Mel's signature model and several others); Buscarino; Benedetto; Gibson (several Johnny Smith models); Fender (their LTD - one of

the most underrated hollowbodies ever); and more. I was in the market for a handmade jazz box and thus played tons of guitars at GMGS. None resonated like Tom's. In fact, even at the time–a time in which Tom, perhaps not even 30, was really getting his business off the ground—it was clear his work was already worthy of placement on the shortlist of legendary luthiers. He had the gift.

Us both being from St. Louis, I was given the opportunity to visit his shop repeatedly, throughout the building process. I was exposed to his artistic and scientific approach. I learned a lot about the way his mind as instrument builder worked and developed a friendship we maintain to this day.

I have since seen him develop innovative nylon and steel string models unparalleled in terms of playability, sonority and visual aesthetics. I have edited his eBook, worked with him on several Mel Bay projects, and more.

It is not often I heap such lavish praise on people; however, Tom is in this case more than deserving: I know of no other luthier whose work I respect more. Tom knows his craft inside and out; he pours his soul into every guitar he makes; he uses cutting-edge science to guide his work, and it shows.

Simply put, I cannot wait to consume this book-and-film package. As head of Artist Relations and Product Development at Mel Bay, it gives me great pleasure to publish Tom's work, which will no doubt take the art of lutherie to a new level. I hope you'll spend some time soaking in this book—it will certainly augment your musicality.

Collin Bay
St. Louis
October, 2013

Acknowledgments

So many people have helped me and made what I do possible, it is impossible to mention them all here. I can only thank a few of you, but even if you weren't mentioned here, you know who you are, and I will always remember that there is no such thing as being "self taught". If I have achieved or go on to achieve anything of significance in my life, it is only because of the people who surrounded, supported, encouraged, instructed, and guided me. Whatever credit may come to me now or in the future, I pass it gratefully along to all of you.

Special thanks to:

Collin Bay
Bob Benedetto
Tom Bills Sr.
John Buscarino
Eugene Clark
Gila Ebon

Boaz Elkyam
Mike King
John Monteleone
Jim Olson
Steph Otis
Roberto Pagnotta

More than anyone else I have to thank my beautiful, loving, and faithful wife Stephanie Bills. Without her none of this would have been possible, and I'm sure I would have self destructed years ago. She stood by me through thick and thin and has encouraged and supported and believed in me and my calling to this craft as a luthier, even when I wasn't so sure myself.

And last but not least, I would like to thank a nurse whose name I don't even know, who when I was diagnosed with never being able to use my hand again after a tragic accident, she cared enough to try to help me, even though I was a total stranger. Her act of kindness enabled me to see a surgeon who was able to reconstruct my hand, when everyone else said it was impossible, giving me a second chance at guitar playing and guitar building. If she didn't take the time to help me that day in the waiting room of the hospital, I wouldn't be writing this today.

Table Of Contents

Preface

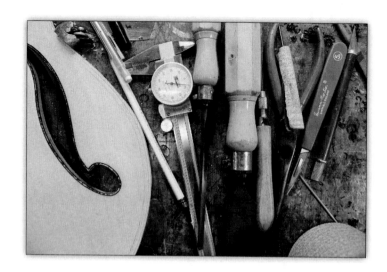

This book is intended to facilitate the beginner or advanced guitar maker in being able to better understand the guitar and its components with the goal of optimizing the responsiveness, playability, and tonality of an instrument. If you have been reading "how-to" books that only tell you how to go through the steps of building a guitar, when what you really want to know is "WHY", this book is the missing piece of the puzzle. Understanding "Why" is vital, not only so you can gain a deeper understanding of why others have developed the systems and techniques that they use, but more importantly, to empower you to make your own educated choices, and create the unique guitars that only you can. The world needs your art, your guitar, your important contribution.

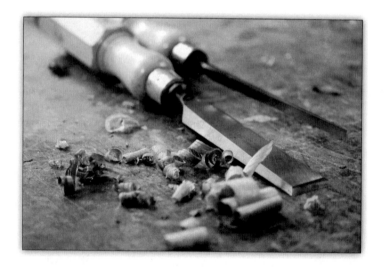

In the following pages I will share with you a collection of my personal techniques and experiences that I currently use when building my guitars. It is my most valuable and cherished tool set that I have been assembling since 1998 when I built my first guitar. Although I make mention many times of theoretical physics and other scientific concepts, it is not my intent that this be a rigorous scientific document, but rather, a tool set built upon practical, experiential knowledge, and tested methods. These methods continue to enable me to not only create my instruments in a way that is deeply satisfying to me, but also have provided me with an effective foundation for continued growth and inspired lutherie in which I am never producing a product, but always creating art that is meaningful to me and my clients.

Introduction

Benefits For The Guitar Player

The guitar player can benefit from this book by developing a deeper and more intimate understanding of his or her instrument. With this greater insight into the guitar itself, the player will not only be able to diagnose and communicate the issues that are preventing the guitar from performing at its fullest potential, but for those who wish to, they can even begin to make adjustments to the guitar themselves.

Also, this new-found enlightenment and demystifying of the physics, and other dynamic principles at play within the system of the guitar, can allow the player to consciously analyze their playing technique and adapt it to a particular guitar. This can assist them in finding the sweet spot on any guitar and developing the sensitivity and consciousness necessary to tap into the very best a guitar has to offer.

Benefits For The Guitar Builder

The guitar builder, regardless of what level of experience they may have, can always benefit from strengthening his or her foundational understanding of the instrument that they build. Every time I teach this material it helps me, even though I have been over it hundreds of times. As we progress through the various stages of development, both personally and in our craft, the same basic information when revisited can reveal new insights as we view it from a new vantage point of higher development each time.

The luthier stands to make invaluable gains in his understanding of why he is making certain choices on his own guitars. Building from a standard blueprint can be a good starting point, but there comes a time when the luthier must look deeper into himself and his craft, and he must attempt to understand the true nature of the principles that are at play in his designs.

By understanding the part that each element of the guitar plays, the luthier gains the ability to make the best choices in design and materials for each guitar. This conscientious and intentional approach to design can empower him to deliver an instrument perfectly suited to a specific player's needs. Many times I am able to drastically alter the tone of a given design to fit the needs of my client by making simple adjustments to the various components and without doing a full redesign of the guitar model itself. This is vital to your success as a custom guitar maker. It is second in importance only to developing your ability to listen. Listen not only to the wood and the guitar, but of equal importance, listen to your customer and correctly translate and connect with them and their needs.

Section One
Designing For Sound

Chapter 1: *Concepts Of Guitar Design*

What Is A Guitar?

This might sound like a strange question at first, but stop and think about it for a moment, do you really know what a guitar is? Is there a hard and fast definition? An instrument with 6 strings maybe? Well, sometimes there are more, sometimes less, so that can't be it.

A fretted instrument with a sound hole in the front? I've seen guitars without frets and without sound holes, and they were still guitars...so that's not it...

OK, bear with me, I'm having a little fun with this idea, but what I'm getting at is this; the guitar seems to be more than just an object that is defined in simple terms, but it IS something specific. I look at it like this: the guitar is what "we" as a culture say it is, it sounds the way "we" think it should, and looks the way "we" say it should look in order to be deemed beautiful or successful in any of the above categories mentioned.

This is important to understand because even though you may consider yourself an artist, you are still taking part in an art form which has a rich history and is very much interwoven into the fabric of our culture globally, as well as many different individual cultures. You are not in a vacuum, so you can put yourself in an advantageous position when you stay grounded on the essential agreed upon definition of the guitar at your given point in history.

In order to keep your work relevant and widely accepted, I find it to be absolutely critical to keep your designs grounded on traditional concepts and within the historically accepted envelope. By all means, push the edges, stretch out, and develop. By all means, express what the guitar is to you! But never forget the origins of the craft and the instrument itself. My guitars look very modern, but woven into the fabric of the design are the foundational concepts and traditional framework of the craft of lutherie that has been passed down for generations.

The guitar, however "we" collectively define it, is and may always be in a constant state of evolution, moving in stride with our cultural tastes and trends. Just as our cultural roots are essential to our progress, so too are the roots of tradition in our treasured craft of lutherie.

Regardless of the style of guitar that one is building - modern or traditional - the principles of physics at play in the given system are the same. The steel strings of an acoustic guitar will have more tension than the nylon strings of a classical guitar. However the curvature of the string is still the same, and requires a similar approach when designing the overall geometry of the guitar and its components in order to obtain the desired tonality and playability to suit the player's needs and the luthier's goals.

The Guitar As A System

The guitar is a unified system consisting of many different components. Each component plays its own unique role in this delicate ecosystem we call the guitar, subtly, and sometimes not so subtly. Each component influences the way this system processes the energy that is input into it by the strings when set in motion by the player.

Very much like any system we encounter in the natural world, every part, no matter how seemingly small or insignificant is still part of the overall whole. Like a small insect plays a vital role in the food chain, so too something as small as a variation in wood density or type can have a profound impact as the chain reaction it initiates is spread and amplified throughout the entire system.

Now we can begin our journey into understanding the guitar and how it functions as a system. We will start by looking at one of the most important aspects of this system. As I mention "the most important aspects of the system" you may have some ideas already as to what it might be, and if you didn't already peek ahead, what would you say it is?

Scale Length

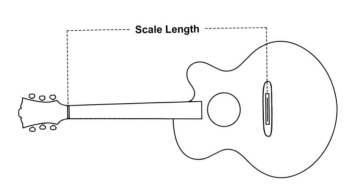

To many guitarists and even guitar builders, the scale length might not seem like the obvious place to start. I typically find that most players and builders alike might begin thinking about a the design of a guitar by looking at the body size or maybe wood choices. While those are definitely important factors, they do not play as important of a role in the system of the guitar as the scale length.

The supreme importance of the guitar's scale length lies in the fact that the scale length acts to alter the harmonic content of the string when it is in motion. When in motion, the guitar string contains within it certain overtones and other harmonic information in the form of vibrational energy. This energy is the initial input that goes directly into the system of the guitar that we will create.

Everything else that happens after the choice of scale length is simply a matter of altering or filtering that initial input. When we choose the scale length we have the opportunity to change the content of the initial input, thus changing the tonal direction of the instrument as we see fit in order to meet the needs of the player. The scale length is the origin from which all other components will be designed around both tonally and physically.

The choice of scale length will have an impact on the comfort of the player as he frets chords and notes on the fingerboard; the size of the player's hand should be also be considered when choosing the scale. However, the tonal implications must be taken into account as well in order to set the initial tonal signature of the guitar, and to ensure that you are beginning your design from an advantageous position.

The Tonal Effects Of Scale Length

When I'm working on a new design for one of my clients, one of the first things I consider is which scale length to use in order to meet the tonal needs of their specific guitar. If I want to give the guitar a smoother, rounder type of tone, I'll choose a shorter scale length because that is the effect that shortening the scale has in the tone of the guitar.

If I want a brighter, more cutting and brilliant type of sound, I'll use a longer scale length for that guitar because having the longer scale length will steer the tonality, or the voice of the guitar, in that direction.

A great way to easily understand this concept for most guitar players and builders is to listen to (or imagine) the sound of a Les Paul guitar, and compare that sound to a Fender Stratocaster. The Les Paul has a short scale, and the Fender Strat has a longer scale. The Les Paul has more mellow trebles and bass notes that are softer and lack focus; these traits are great for specific types of music. On the other hand, the Fender Strat has more focused and cutting trebles and clearer, tighter bass notes, which of course are great for other applications.

So why does the scale length of the guitar change the tonal makeup of the string energy that is present within the string? The full answer to that question is beyond what science can currently explain accurately, but in essence, it has to do with the specific length of each string, the diameter of the string, and the pitch to which the string is tuned. These main factors, as well as others, are all interacting with the string's ability to divide itself into the overtone series relative to the fundamental note, or the main pitch of the string.

Harmonic Content of an Open E String

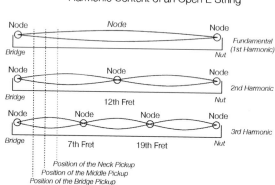

The fundamental note is like the root note of a chord. It gives the note its identity. The actual makeup of a single note is similar in many ways to a chord. It has a fundamental or a "root" that gives it its name. A single note also has a series of higher frequency components that act to give the note its distinctive qualities much in the same way that the higher notes of a chord will give the chord its qualities of major, minor, dominant, etc. The higher frequencies or "overtones" present within a single note don't make it major or minor, but they do determine the qualities of the note such as whether it sounds bright, dark, sharp, round, or any of the myriad of words we use as we attempt to describe what we are perceiving as we listen to a musical note.

Early on in my building career I was fortunate to discover and develop the ability to hear this microcosm within each note, which helped me greatly to gauge how effectively the choices I was making in my designs were working. I realized that I could listen to the single notes of each string, actually "listening inside the note" as I eventually began to call it. I found that I could somewhat tune the overtones of the string in a way.

Most guitars I hear have a struggle happening within the notes. It reminds me of a singer who works extremely hard to sing. They sweat, and they struggle, and they push that note out with all their might. On the other end of the spectrum, the note that is at peace or in tune within, rings out with ease. This also reminds me of a singer, but in this case, one who makes it seem effortless, one who just lets the power and the beauty of their voice, their gift, out for the world to enjoy. A very different experience as a listener, as a singer, and as a player of a guitar that is truly in tune.

You will likely find me talking about the "voice" of a guitar, or comparing things to a singer quite a bit throughout this book, and I want to take a moment to point out why I see it that way. I feel that the guitar should be almost a living thing, as close to alive as we as can create. In order for this to happen, we must change our way of thinking from the guitar as something that makes sounds, to a type of receiver, almost a kind of generator. Like our heart generates the power for our body and draws the electricity it uses to fire neurons and other electrical systems from some other place, the guitar must have that breath, and that life spark, as each component of the guitar effortlessly and harmoniously processes that power it receives from the player's hands and heart, resulting in the guitar's true voice. Not just a sound, there is a huge difference between a sound and a voice.

Creating a guitar that has notes that sing can be much easier when we stop to listen inside the notes, and help the overtones and the fundamental notes to find a place of rest, peace, and harmony by the subtle choices we make while building and setting up the guitar.

Yes, I'm getting a little deep, but I feel strongly that the craft of guitar making is in danger of losing its depth and its richness, especially in the more subtle and sensitive areas such as this. We have to preserve that special part of making a musical instrument that is so different from any other object, it is sacred in a way. I consider myself blessed beyond measure that I was privileged to be in the right places at the right times, to learn this vital aspect of guitar making that not only revolutionized my guitars and the way I create them, but literally transformed every aspect of my life and enriched the way I view the world.

So now that we have discussed the vital importance of the scale length as it pertains to the guitar's voice and tonal character, we will continue to look deeper into why the different scales affect the strings tonally as they do. Keep in mind as we continue our talk about scale length and specifically this next part about how the string is either encouraged or discouraged to divide itself into the different components of the overtone series for its pitch, that the same concepts will also affect the top of the guitar as it is set in motion.

Fanned Frets - Multi-Scale

After discussing how important the scale length can be in getting the right tone from your guitar you might be thinking about the fact that when you make the scale shorter you get better trebles but less focused and slower basses. When you make the scale longer you get brittle and piercing trebles but wonderfully strong and clear bass notes. It's a little frustrating to always have to compromise, but what if you want the best of both worlds?

The good news is that you CAN have your cake and eat it too, or should I say; you can have great trebles AND basses too. You can have the best of all worlds in one guitar with Fan Frets. By using multiple scale lengths on the same fingerboard you can have the longer scales on the bass strings to keep them at their best and make them work better for dropped tuning as well. You can also use the shorter scales for the higher strings to keep the notes round and sweet. Not only is that great, but the best part is that doing this actually makes the guitar more comfortable to play as well. The added comfort is a result of the multi scale or Fan Fret arrangement being more ergonomic due to the fact that the splay of the resulting fret positions more closely match the angles that the fingers naturally fan out in when you spread your fingers.

There is no downside, maybe other than making the instrument harder to build due to the added complexity. Once you try it a few times, it gets easier and the results are simply stunning. Once I tried a fan fret for the first time, I have never wanted to play anything but a fan fret ever since.

Tip
If using fan frets be sure to lay out your fret spacing for each scale along actual string path lines and not the edges of the fingerboard. I find it good practice in general when laying out any fingerboard, to start with the string spacing I want and then measure out from there to establish the edges of the fingerboard, rather than the other way around.

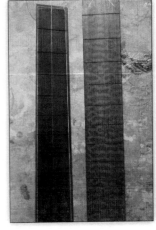

The intonation of the fan fret guitar works the same way with the same challenges and solutions for overcoming Enharmonicity and achieving perfect intonation and action.

Chapter 2: *Defining The Rules Of The Game*

We looked closely at the length of the strings, now let's turn our focus toward the string itself and how it behaves. In your mind visualize that string at rest. One single string of a set length held under tension so that it is tuned to the desired pitch. As we discuss the information to follow try to imagine that string and see its behavior. Up until now we have only talked about the length of the string in this resting state, but there are other aspects of our design that will be significant factors in shaping the string's behavior, and ultimately its tone and quality of sound. Once the string is put in motion, there are several foundational concepts and rules of behavior that every component of the guitar will follow. They are the rules of the game, and by understanding them, we can play the game more effectively, have more fun, and win more often.

Effects Of Thickness

The first factor we will talk about is the string gauge or thickness and how it affects the behavior of the string in motion. Understanding this concept is crucial to creating an instrument that is in tune, but also, as we will discover in later parts of our journey, this same concept will apply to nearly every component of the guitar.

When a guitar string or any object becomes thicker, I find that it functionally becomes stiffer, or more specifically of interest to us, harder to bend into small pieces. The analogy that finally drove the point home for me was when one of my mentors and my good friend, luthier Gila Eban, explained it with the following analogy: If we were to take a piece of paper and fold it in half once it would be relatively easy to fold. Then we could fold it in half again and still it might fold nicely, but as we continue to fold it in half, each time it becomes more difficult as the new portion being folded becomes thicker. As the thickness increases, the ability to easily fold or bend the paper in half becomes more difficult. Another important thing to note is that in our paper example, not only is it more difficult to fold in half as the thickness increases, but if we wanted to fold it into extremely small pieces it can become literally impossible due to the increasing thickness. If the paper was laid out flat with no folds at all, folding it into smaller pieces, let's say 1" sections would be quite easy.

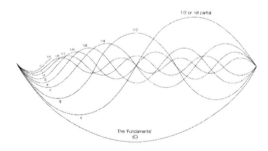

The reason this concept is important is not because we are going to do some origami with our guitar components or strings, but because when a string is in motion after being plucked by the player, it immediately begins dividing itself into smaller and smaller pieces, as much as the scale and the thickness will allow. By 'smaller pieces' I'm referring to vibration patterns with smaller distances between nodes (and antinodes). These correspond to higher harmonics or higher partials. In other words, this dividing of the string, and the sound board, as it vibrates is what shapes it's overtones, or harmonics, thereby producing the different qualities of the string's tonal character that we perceive.

For the guitar string, this means that the thinner the string, the more 'small' vibrations, or folds, the string is capable of producing. You might have guessed by now that what I mean when I say, 'smaller vibrations' are really 'higher harmonics'. As the frequency gets higher, the size of the physical wave for that frequency gets smaller and so does the section of the string that it must divide into when producing it.

Tempo

Right now I'm building a guitar for my client and friend who is a master of a Japanese flute called the shakuhachi. If you have ever heard that instrument, you will know that it is played with great patience and space between the notes. It is deeply transporting and peaceful music.

Because he shared this with me along with his vision for the voice of his guitar, I am building an instrument for him with a similar depth and breath in response, and a slower, deeper tempo to its voice. Not like a flamenco guitar that explodes all at once like the flamenco singer's voice, but a longer sustaining, ringing breath to the full, round notes.

The voice of the guitar itself has a tempo, and once you experience it, you can begin to set this tempo to match the playing style of your clients or when building your own guitar. If you are a player, then maybe you might begin to more consciously hear and understand this attribute in the guitars you play and are drawn to. Understanding the tempo of the guitar will help you to more fully bring out all that this guitar has to offer in its own unique way as you create your music with it. It is just one more way to get in sync with the instrument so it can become more transparent allowing your music to flow freely.

Frequency

Frequency has to do with cycles per second, with time. I personally find the guitar string fascinating in its amazing complexity when it is in motion. It's like a time machine existing in multiple dimensions at once. Each frequency moving at a different speed, and if the guitar is set up and intonated correctly, the different frequencies are all in tune together like a symphony of parallel universes singing together in harmony.

When we take this same concept and apply it to the soundboard or other components of the guitar, we can see that making, for example, a thinner soundboard, will set up a situation in which the higher partials—or smaller vibrations—are able to find a home with less resistance. Having less resistance means that a situation is present in which those frequencies can exist more efficiently. It's easier for them to "fold" the soundboard into smaller size pieces. Conversely, a thicker soundboard will discourage 'smaller pieces', or higher partials, and encourage the 'larger pieces' corresponding to the fundamental and lower partials.

Before I get too far off into how this applies to the soundboard or other components of the guitar body itself which we will do later on, we need to look at another aspect of the gauge or string thickness as it affects the string's behavior. We now know that as any object, in our case a guitar string, becomes thicker it effectively becomes stiffer or harder to bend. We also talked a lot about how this affects the totality of the string in that a thicker string will discourage higher frequencies, but there is another effect caused by increasing thickness and the resulting increase of stiffness; in a way... it shrinks!

Enharmonicity And Compensation

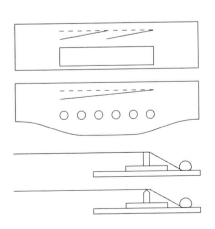

The second effect we find that results from a thicker guitar string is called Enharmonicity. Yes, it is a particularly fancy word and it is great for impressing your friends, but all joking aside, I'm sure you are wondering, "what does it mean?"

To illustrate this effect, let's think of a standard wound steel guitar string that is 25.125" long with a string gauge of .053" (This is commonly used for the low E string on an acoustic guitar). Even though the length of this string from nut to saddle is 25.125, it will have a true vibrating length of about only 25"; this phenomenon is known as Enharmonicity. You may have guessed already that the Enharmonicity of a guitar string is related to its gauge. What creates the shrinking of the true vibrating length of the string is the fact that because it is thicker, it becomes stiffer. The extra stiffness, relative to a thinner string like that of the High E string measuring only about .012" causes the tiny bits of string just as it leaves the nut and the saddle to lose their ability to vibrate, thus shortening the actual vibrating length of the string. Because of this we are forced to lengthen what we can call the "measured length" of the string. We do this by offsetting the saddle of the guitar until the actual "vibrating length" of the string is correct to compensate for Enharmonicity. Adding this extra length is known as "Compensation".

This is a very important concept to have a firm grasp on when building guitars as it relates to your design. Ensuring that your guitar will sound perfectly in tune as each string is allowed to vibrate at the proper actual vibrating length despite the effects of differences in string gauges.

Tension

A third effect of the larger gauge is that each time we increase it, we also increase the amount of tension that must be applied on the string in order to reach a target pitch. This is one of the main reasons that we use thicker strings for the lower tuned strings of the guitar. Since the string is tuned to a lower note, we don't want it to be floppy and feel loose as we play, so by increasing the gauge, we can increase the amount of tension in that string. As well as giving the string a better feel for the player, it will also encourage the lower frequencies and discourage the higher overtones of the strings.

Anatomy Of The String

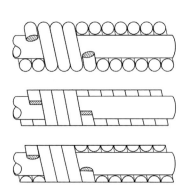

As a side note, you may have wondered why the strings with lower open tuning notes of the guitar are wrapped with wire. Wrapping the string with wire or what we refer to as "round wound", "flat wound", or just simply a "wound string", is a brilliant solution, literally. It allows the string to be thicker, which has the desired effects that we mentioned earlier, but at the same time, because the core of the string is thin and the wrappings, while touching each other, are not connected to one another, the string as a whole retains a great deal of flexibility. This extra flexibility gives the string more definition in the upper frequencies. Added flexibility also minimizes the amount of compensation necessary to counteract the Enharmonicity while maintaining the correct physical vibrating length in order for the string to be in tune properly with the other strings of the guitar.

String Theory & The Blueprint For Sound

We have been dedicating our focus thus far in this book to the guitar string itself. To me, the physics of the string in motion are a great conceptual tool in easily understanding the way all the parts of the guitar will behave when in motion. The same approach and treatments that I apply to the strings, I use as the basis of the way I approach and treat the other components of the guitar. My intent is to illustrate the forces at play using the string, and this "string theory" approach, which can then be applied to the rest of the guitar in order to systematically optimize and control the behavior of individual components, as well as the final outcome of the overall system.

The guitar will not create an exact copy of the string, a computer could do that, but the guitar system we create will add its own unique character and responsiveness to the signal of the string, processing it as we have programmed it to do by our design choices, material selections, and techniques. If we have done our job right, the wooden guitar will change the guitar string's input from a sound into a voice, and only then will it become a musical instrument.

Through fully understanding the behavior and nuances of the string in motion, we are able to construct the rest of the guitar such that it will be able to mimic the same behavior efficiently. The string itself is also a simplified model of the nature of the physics that we are dealing with in the production of sound from a physical object. The guitar string itself is the perfect thing to study, and by understanding it, we can rest assured that we have a firm foundation from which the rest of our guitar design can be built around in an appropriate, efficient, and unified manner.

Continuing in this line of thought, we also talked about the physical properties or the structure of the string, but our main focus must always be the vibration, or the behavior of the string; the sound over the structure. I feel that far too many people focus on the structure of the guitar. They design it like they are designing a house. Yes, there are some parallels to architecture, but the guitar is not just a building or an object to be pretty (though the true nature of beauty contains within it the same concepts of harmony as the string) but, the guitar is a receiver. It receives the vibrating string energy, and it reacts, but it also receives input from the player. This is obvious as you hear the same guitar played by two different people. The difference is striking even if the level of skill is nearly the same, the tonal result of the guitar is totally different because the human element, the life that we breathe into it as players and as builders is at the heart of this interaction and should be understood at least intuitively and factored into the creation of the guitar.

Doing so will help the builder to create art, to make something meaningful that conveys a message, a feeling, an experience which is what the guitar is about. The guitar should not be like a product, or a building, or even a statue. A good guitar is all of those things, but a truly exceptional guitar is alive and has a voice too.

Creating A Full Scale Drawing

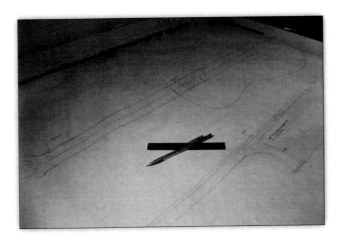

I strongly believe in drawing each new model of guitar. I make a full scale drawing which will force me to work out each element of design in real units of measure and also provide a historical record I can refer to as I build now, and also in the future. If you don't have a blueprint, then you will find yourself wasting time calculating important dimensions and other critical components multiple times as you build. This is dangerous because every time you recalculate, you open yourself up to an increased likelihood of errors as well as waste more time. However, you can avoid much of this by simply taking the time at the beginning and making a drawing, calculate, recheck, and then rest assured that everything is correct. It is also very important to actually write each dimension on the drawing. Due to changes in humidity, a large piece of paper or even vellum will change dimension relative to the atmospheric conditions. Having the original and intended measurements written down will ensure that your work will stay accurate even if the drawing itself should be physically altered by the hygroscopic nature of the material.

Having said the previous statements about drawing a blueprint, I think it is essential to add that I take many liberties as I'm building. It is a little like our discussion on keeping our designs, no matter how radical outwardly, rooted in tradition. A radical design needs a solid foundation to stand on or else it loses its validity and frame of reference. In this case the blueprint you create can be the foundation you work off of, taking your creative liberties while knowing you have the underlying structure and geometry intact. When the guitar calls for changes in order to be its best, I'll make them, all the while recording things in my notes, building my database, and adding to my collective pool of experiential knowledge I'm amassing to go along with it and add real world validity to the blueprints themselves.

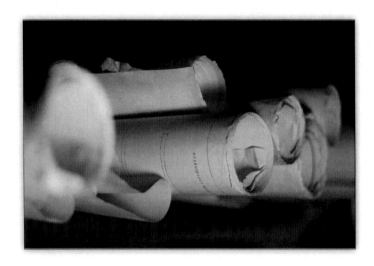

The blueprints you draw will also help you build "intentionally". What I mean is that every component must have a measure. No part of the guitar should ever be random, or "close enough". In my experience, the best guitars are always organized and executed with precision, even the components no one will ever see. I can assure you, if you listen closely, you will hear it in the final guitar, so take the time to make them accurate and intentional. Having the blueprint will help you to quickly see what the tail block, for example, should measure so you can create it as drawn. This is crucial because like the overtones of the string that must be in tune and not fighting one another, so too, all components of the guitar must be in tune dimensionally so as to create the best possible situation for harmony in both sound and vision.

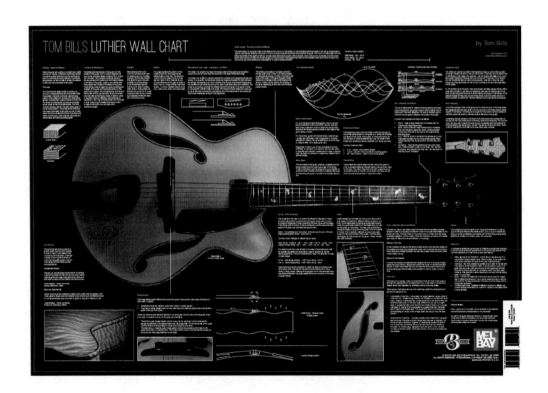

Also available from Mel Bay
"MB30360 Tom Bills Luthier Wall Chart"

16

Section Two
Application Of Principals

Now that we have looked at the physics and interactions between the different main elements of the guitar strings, we can shift our attention to the application of this new understanding in order to get the most from our instrument by optimizing the main components of the guitar system.

Rather than moving from this point right into talking about the overall structure of the guitar and its design in detail, I feel it is best to keep moving in that direction, but in smaller and specifically chosen steps. The next incremental and essential concept to understand is the setup and neck geometry of the guitar.

Chapter 3: *Set Up & Geometry*

Most people may think about the setup of the guitar after the fact: after it is made, then you set it up, right? It is easy to think that the set up just makes the action lower and makes it play more comfortably. Some people do not even seem to care much about the setup at all. I can tell when I play a guitar like that because the strings are tight and stiff, and the intonation is usually terrible. The guitar is fighting against itself and the player! There is no peace inside the notes, just a turbulent sea of physical and harmonic discord.

For me and my guitars, the setup is a vital and critical point that the rest of the guitar is designed around, second only to the choice of scale length. I start with the string, then I move to the setup and the geometry of the way the string interacts with the fingerboard, the bridge, and the player.

In order to create the best possible setup we have to look closely at each of the important elements involved in the guitar's setup and how each of these elements interact with one another and the player. Since we have been focusing on the behavior of the guitar strings quite a bit, I think it would be a natural next step to look at the strings' interaction with the fingerboard and frets.

Action: String-Fingerboard Interaction

The action of the guitar is the term most commonly used to describe the distance between the strings and the fret surfaces. When we "set up" the guitar we are setting the action. Because it is the first thing a player experiences as he or she plays the guitar, the feel of the action will create the first impression the player has and may greatly influence the overall opinion of the guitar. Learning to properly set the action so that it is optimized for comfort as well as responsiveness and tonal richness, starts with understanding the interaction and geometry of the fingerboard and the strings.

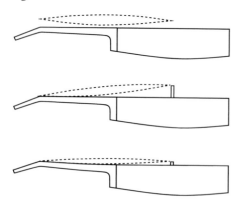

When we think of a guitar string, we usually imagine a thin straight line. In reality, the effect of gravity acting on the string's own weight is pulling on the string, giving it a certain natural type of curve. This shape is similar to the curve we observe in many different places in nature. This is the curve you must become intimately acquainted with if you want to be able to reach the pinnacle of your potential as a luthier in setup, as well as increase the tonal and visual harmony of your guitars. This curve imparted on the string from gravity is also related to the shape induced into the string as it is vibrating.

To find this curve simply walk outside and look up at some nearby power lines. Those power lines are much like a guitar string. They are steel cables stretched under pressure between two points. You will immediately see the gentle curve induced into the power line cables by the force of gravity pulling down on them.

Now that you have that shape in your mind, you can transfer that shape in your mind's eye to the guitar string in motion. This shape of the guitar string in motion, with its natural curve, will be your guide as you design and execute the contour of your guitar's fingerboard and fretwork.

The Fingerboard

The shape or bow of the fingerboard must interact with the string very intimately and together they must act in harmony and be in sync with one another. This relationship is essential for the feel of the guitar to be the best it can possibly be, but also for the tone of the guitar to be optimized as well.

Often times I will hear a noticeable improvement in a guitar just by correctly setting this relationship between the strings and the fingerboard. I can't say that I fully understand (not from a scientific standpoint anyway) why having the nut slot depth just right, and the fingerboard curve in a certain place, produces such an improvement. All I can tell you is that when these elements are in sync you will hear and feel the improvement on any guitar. The interesting thing is that there is not a magic formula for creating this situation, it is subtly different for every guitar.

Because this seemingly elusive relationship between strings, fingerboard, nut slot depth, and saddle height are always changing, the most valuable skill to develop is the ability to track down and recognize this when you find it. The important concepts that we have covered up to this point will act as your tool kit, enabling you to analyze the situation present on whatever guitar you may be dealing with, and focus in on the problem that needs to be corrected in order to bring the guitar into its optimal state. This will serve you far better than memorizing a set of measurements for a given type of guitar to simply repeat each time you set up a guitar.

Forward Bow Of The Fingerboard

Understanding the shape of the string in motion gives us a blueprint for how the fingerboard must be shaped to enable the player to have low action and still prevent the strings from buzzing against the frets. The easiest way I have found to replicate the natural arc that a string takes when in motion is to take a flexible steel rule at least 24" long (you could use wood if it has an even flexibility from end to end) and push in on each end forcing the center to bow outwardly. The resulting shape is an arc similar to the natural curve of the string. Notice that the twelfth fret will be the center of the string, dividing it in half, and as such, the widest point of oscillation for the string. The shape of the fingerboard forward bow should have its deepest point around this area. Many builders either make a flat fingerboard surface when building the guitar, resulting in a particularly odd surface after the neck bows forward from string tension.

Another common mistake is to think of the arc (forward bow) as if it were from one end of the fingerboard to the other which would move the deepest point up toward the nut and to the center of the neck, which is not the same as the center of the string and also results in less than perfect action and tone.

I find it best to design the forward bow into the neck shaft itself. When preparing the neck blank to receive the fingerboard, I add this curve subtly to its surface. I also include a slight bit of extra curve because I typically use a water based glue for this joint and the water in the glue will cause a bit of back bow during the gluing process.

Fretwork

The fretwork on a guitar is of utmost importance because each fret is the point that the string is joined to the guitar. The vibrational energy in the string must be solidly isolated into the proper length set by the fret placement. This solid grounding caused by the left hand fretting of the string is essential for optimal efficiency, responsiveness, and quality of tone.

Fingerboard Radius

Before your frets can be installed in the fingerboard, its surface must be shaped with a radius that fits the playing style and tastes of the player for whom you are creating the guitar. I have not noticed any difference in tone using different radii, so this is simply a matter of the players preference.

I might be jumping ahead a little bit, but I want to also take a moment to talk about the relationship between the fingerboard radius and the fret surface radius. On my guitars, I only put a single radius on the fingerboard surface. I commonly use a 16" fingerboard radius for my steel strings and archtops. I will use this all along the fingerboard before I put in my frets. I use a shorter radius block so I can make sure I keep that little bit of forward bow I was discussing earlier. This single radius produces a surface similar to a cylinder which is fairly easy to create using a radius sanding block. The problem is that the strings are not traveling along this surface parallel to the virtual cylinder's center line. Instead, the strings are traveling across the surface at different angles. To compensate for this, it is essential that after your frets are in place, you use a straight file or abrasive paper to grind off the tops of the frets in line with the lay of each string path. This has the effect of changing the surface from that of a simple cylinder to what is known as a compound radius. This compound radius is more of a subtle cone shape which will enable the curve of the string to function properly as it interacts with the fret surface.

Choosing Fret Wire

When selecting fret wire for a guitar, you should consider a few different important elements to help you select the appropriate wire for the guitar. The first of which is the size of the bead or the fret height and width.

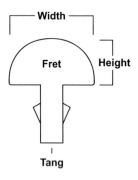

Fret Size

The fret size will affect two things:

1. The first is intonation. The thinner the fret wire, the more precise the intonation, and the wider the wire, the less accurate.

2 Secondly, the fret size will also affect the mass of the wire. Increasing mass (size) will make the anchoring of the string when fretted more efficient with less wasted energy leaking into the fret and fingerboard. This keeps more string energy in the vibrating portion of the string and has the effect of increasing sustain. The thinner wire will have less mass and will not increase the sustain, but will give the guitar a more acoustic and brighter sound in my experience.

Fret Material

The second thing to consider in choice of fret wire is the material or the makeup of the wire itself. A harder wire like stainless steel will sound extremely cold and bright and feel slippery and easy to bend strings on for the player. The softer metals have more of a grip to them and tend to warm up the tone a little bit. This is one of those subtle things that unless you hear the two different frets on the same guitar it may be hard to piece together the tonal changes you are perceiving. I can tell you from my experience though, replacing standard nickel silver frets with stainless steel makes a huge difference in the tone and feel of the guitar. For some guitars, this difference can be good, but for others it could ruin the sound. So choose the material that will be best suited for the goals you have in mind for each guitar. I usually prefer a softer nickel silver 18% wire for the tone I am aiming toward on most of my guitars.

The Crown

The last part of the fret wire to discuss is the crown (see Fret Diagram in previous section). The crown of the fret is the shape of the part of the wire that is above the fingerboard and that interacts with the guitar string when fretted. For accurate intonation, it is essential to make a nice evenly rounded shape with the highest point of the curve exactly over the centerline of the fret slot. This keeps the point of contact for the string in the correct location to divide the string properly and allow it to be in tune with the other strings and with itself.

Fret Ends

Fret ends must be smoothly rounded and fit to the fingerboard. This is critical to the guitar feeling comfortable to the player. If the fret ends are not well fit and shaped now, over time they can pop up and leave sharp uncomfortable edges of the fingerboard. It is also advisable to use ebony for your fingerboard that has been seasoned for as long as possible. If you can not season it in your shop for several years, you can sometimes use a regular clothes iron to heat it and shrink it dimensionally, using a caliper to measure its changes after each heating session. A fingerboard that was not seasoned long enough will eventually shrink and leave the pointy ends of the frets sticking out along the neck. It is also true that no matter how long an ebony fingerboard is seasoned, or heated, after many many years in a dry climate, the ebony may still shrink a bit. Taking time to season the fingerboard thoroughly before building can at least delay and minimize the potential for a noticeable dimensional change in the ebony for many many years.

Neck Angle

The neck angle or back set of the guitar neck in relation to the guitar's body is very critical in setting the amount of tension that will be exerted on the top of the guitar through the bridge. It also can affect how much tension the player will feel in the strings as they play. This aspect of your design must be considered before you ever start building as it will greatly change the way that you build the top of the guitar.

A guitar with a greater degree of back-set will put more force on the bridge, because of this, the top of the guitar will need to be thicknessed and braced accordingly to handle that tension and designed to process it sonically to get the tonal effect you desire. A guitar with less back-set will put less pressure on the guitar top and the guitar must then be built in a way that it is sensitive enough to respond well to the lighter tension load.

In general a guitar with too much tension resulting from too much neck back-set angle will sound choked with muted basses. A guitar with too little tension will usually have excessive and unfocused bass and weak trebles. These are general statements because so many other things play into the scenario because the guitar is a complex and interconnected system.

Some of the factors to consider when deciding on the neck back-set angle would be the scale length and how much tension it will add, the string gauge, the lightness or stiffness of the top and its bracing, the desired bridge height and its effect on the tonality and response, as well as other aspects.

As always, start from the traditional standards and experiment to see what works best for your design, approach, and clients.

Elevated Fingerboard

I think it is worth mentioning the elevated fingerboard type of design while we are talking about the neck angle. When I think of this element of design, I'm really attracted to it because of the tonal improvements I have experienced from using it. It was a natural progression for me because I began my career as a luthier building only archtop guitars all of which have a type of elevated fingerboard. I first used it on a guitar other than an archtop because a customer requested it and the only real advantage I saw at that time was having more control over the fingerboard and neck angle without having to alter the top of the guitar, as well as providing the player with easier access to

fretting the upper frets with the left hand. After building the guitar however, I instantly fell in love with the way it affected the sound of the guitar. Ever since I have made it a standard part of my nylon and steel string guitar designs.

I think it looks a bit funny to have the neck leaning forward too much, so when I do an elevated fingerboard, I slope the top down to accommodate the thickness of the fingerboard as it extends over the guitar body. This has a wonderful side effect that I think is improving the sound in a very good way.

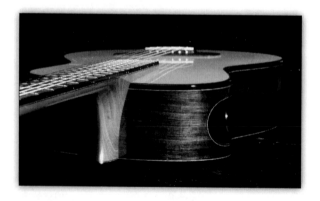

Because the top is sloping down it changes the angle of approach of the strings in relation to the plane of the soundboard. It seems to add a more harp-like tonality to the notes, a rounder and more pure quality. My theory (and it is just that) is that the harp has the strings approaching from a very steep angle. This changes the way the torque of the strings are acting on the soundboard. Adding the elevated fingerboard to my guitars seems to have added a more harp-like purity to the notes, it's subtle, but it was a noticeable improvement to me.

Break Over Angle

In the case of the archtop guitar the effects of the neck angle that we mentioned above can be greatly fine tuned by changing the break over angle of the tailpiece. The break over angle is the angle that the string leaves the saddle and then moves back toward the top of the guitar. Fine tuning this angle by reducing it can open up and balance out an under built guitar. By increasing this angle it can balance and bring life into a slightly overbuilt guitar.

Raising the tailpiece can also help reduce the tension that a player experiences as they fret the strings. This can be very helpful in fine tuning the feel of the strings to meet an individual player's tastes.

Chapter 4: *Main Components*

Once the neck geometry and fretwork have been designed to accomplish our tonal and structural goals, we can move to the next step in the system of the guitar—the bridge.

The bridge is one of the most critical parts of the guitar because it is the transducer that converts the string vibration into a form of energy that the top of the guitar can effectively work with and understand.

There are two main types of guitar bridge systems that are commonly used. They are quite different, but they both in their own way accomplish the goal of translating the string energy into a waveform understood by the soundboard.

Steel String Bridge

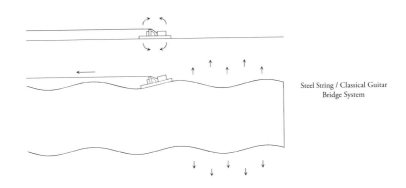

Steel String / Classical Guitar
Bridge System

The first type of bridge is the steel string or acoustic guitar bridge. On this type of bridge, the strings are anchored into the bridge, or through the bridge to the inside of the guitar just behind the saddle. The bridge itself is glued permanently to the guitar's top. The anchoring of the strings into the bridge itself determines how the bridge will behave when the strings are in motion.

If you picture a string in motion, as we discussed in earlier chapters, it moves in a long arc at its widest oscillation. We compared this arc to other similar natural curves induced by gravity such as what we see when we look at high voltage power lines. We see this natural arc in many different places in nature. In fact, you can even take your shop ruler and press in on each end, the resulting natural curve will be the same shape as the string in motion.

Let's do a thought experiment: Picture a string at rest, stretched between two points. Measure it from one end to the other, suppose the distance is 25". Now picture the same string frozen in time at the moment of its widest oscillation, its largest vibration and curve. If we measure that string again the distance from end to end will be slightly shorter than the same string in a resting state. This is because when the center portion of the string moves outward from the resting state location, its increased tension pulls the ends of the strings toward each other with greater force causing the measured length of the string to be less. It is similar to pushing in on the ends of your shop ruler, causing it to bend. The length of the ruler doesn't change, but you are shortening the distance between its ends in order to get the right curve along its length and move it outward at its center point.

Right now we are talking about the type of bridge used on a steel string acoustic guitar which has the strings anchored through the bridge and to the inside of the guitar through the bridge-pin holes. Because of this arrangement, the shortening of the string each time it oscillates causes the bridge to be pulled up behind the saddle where the strings are anchored. The bridge then begins to rock forward and back in concert with the string oscillation, thus driving the soundboard with a wave form that resembles the motion of the strings' vibrational waveform. In reality, the bridge's actual motion is quite complicated and not limited to rocking forward and backward. In my experience however, it is most practical when designing the soundboard to focus mainly on the rocking bridge motion.

A properly designed guitar will have a structure which harnesses the rocking action of the bridge in the most efficient way possible. The goal is usually to obtain maximum conversion of vibrational string energy to soundboard motion. The tone bars can be arranged in different patterns in order to harness the bridge motion in order to shape the type of frequencies and modes of vibration you want to encourage or discourage in the behavior of the guitar top.

Archtop Bridge

Archtop Bridge System

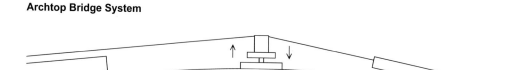

The bridge of the archtop guitar is related to that of the violin family of instruments in which the strings are not anchored into the bridge itself, but are attached to the instrument at a tailpiece. This arrangement changes the way that the string energy is translated into the form of motion that can couple with the top of the guitar and then be converted to audible sound. When the string tries to shrink or contract each time it reaches maximum oscillation, it is prevented from rocking the bridge, at least to the extent that it does with the steel string guitar because the strings are anchored into the tailpiece, which in turn is solidly anchored to the end block of the guitar.

The effect of this limiting of the string motion by the tailpiece is that the bridge tends to move in more of an up and down, pumping motion, somewhat akin to that of a trampoline. With the violin, this motion is further encouraged by the use of a sound-post inside the instrument. The violin bridge must pivot like a seesaw, up and down over the sound-post, creating a situation where the widest motion of the bridge is on the furthest tip of the bass side of the bridge. This is an optimal setup since the bass frequencies will have a longer wavelength and thus need a larger range of motion by the bridge in order to accurately reproduce those frequencies.

This is not to say that the bass frequencies must only be localized on the bass side of the instrument soundboard though, in most cases, the bass frequencies need the whole sound board to move in a balanced symmetrical mode in order to be produced effectively.

The Sound Board

So far in this text we have talked a great deal about the guitar string and we have used it as our centerpiece of design for understanding and engineering the setup, playability, and tone of the guitar. Now that we understand this core aspect of the machine we know and love as the guitar, we can turn our focus to the top or the sound-board, and how the string and its energy and behavior interact to drive its motion.

The soundboard itself is a plate of wood that is intentionally thicknessed to respond in a specific way to the vibration induced through the bridge. Before we can get very deep into the design and architecture of the soundboard itself, we need to look at the different supporting elements that facilitate the soundboard's action and shape its behavior.

Linings and Recurve

In order for the top of the guitar to be able to function at its maximum or desired potential, careful attention must be put into the design and execution of the boundary areas around the perimeter of the guitar body, specifically where the top is attached to the sides of the guitar. The design of this area can greatly influence the behavior of the top, and encourage or discourage certain behaviors or the frequency-response characteristics, optimizing responsiveness of the guitar.

Diving Board

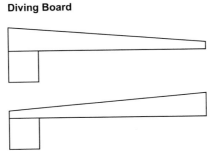

The best analogy I know of to help explain clearly what is happening at this important intersection between the top and side of the guitar is that of a diving board. The diving board has two main components, the board and the base. The board is similar in function and behavior to the top of the guitar. Try to visualize the way the diving board would flex and respond to someone jumping on it if it were thicker near the base and thinner near the tip. Try to see the way the energy is being dispersed and utilized throughout the board itself as well as through its base. Next, visualize how it might respond to someone jumping on it if it were thinner near the base and thicker near the tip. You can probably see in your mind's eye that it would be quite a different response from the one depicted in the previous case where the board's tip is thinner.

Recurve

The diving board with the thinnest portion near the tip is going to favor higher frequency motions in the thinner areas, but because of the extremely thick region near the base, a large portion of the board won't bend at all, or will bend very little. The thicker area near the diving board's base has the same effect as the stiffness of a string near its anchor-points. When speaking of a guitar string this is called enharmonicity, a similar concept applies here when dealing with the sound board. If the guitar is 16" wide across the lower bout and the soundboard is overly stiff near the perimeter, the actual vibrating surface that is usable has a width that is smaller than 16".

For the other design of the diving board with the thicker portion near the tip and the thinnest portion near the base, you might already be guessing by now that this design will be the opposite of the first design. This type will encourage the lower frequencies and create a slower, more floppy type of response and behavior when energized. The thicker tip literally can not divide itself efficiently into sections that are small enough to produce the shorter, higher frequency wavelengths. This type of situation will maximize the length of the board that can be utilized, and have less of an effect of shortening the usable vibrating area of the piece. This is similar to the way the thinner guitar string behaves, resulting in an actual vibrating length that is closer to the actual physical length of the string. Because the area near the tip of the diving board is so thick, it cannot produce higher frequencies well, and the overall behavior will be mostly lower frequencies and a slower response.

With this analogy in mind, we can engineer the response and frequency bias of the top by the way we thickness the sound board in order to control and balance its behavior. Most factory guitars have a soundboard that is an even thickness throughout. I should also note that the differences in thickness we are talking about here are very small and for most steel string and nylon string guitars will not vary more than about .5mm or .020". On an Archtop guitar there can be more variation. Sometimes there can be as much as 3mm or .120" difference from the thickest portion in the center to the thinnest at the recurve area.

How much you choose to vary the thickness of the top is up to you and you must experiment in order to understand the effects and find your own path.

You can also experiment with how you blend or "graduate" these different thicknesses into one another. Or in other words, how fast or slow you transition from the thickest size to the thinnest. I have had good results in smoothly and subtly flowing the thinnest areas usually near the edges, out toward the thickest area near the bridge location, but I subtly vary each guitar to get the response I need for each client and to compensate for wood variations in stiffness and density.

As you consider the thickness of the soundboard and other parts of the guitar, it is essential to keep in mind just how thickness relates to stiffness. It's really quite amazing to me how much stiffness is lost by sanding or in some way removing a very small amount of wood.

You can find more scientific information by searching for the Cube Rule Of Stiffness to learn more about the effects of stiffness and thickness. As with all this information, make your final decisions for adjusting the thicknesses of the soundboard and other components with your heart and your ears as you intuitively assess the needs of the guitar you are building. You can use the scientific and analytical part of your brain later, but now when you are voicing the guitar top in this way, it's time to perform, just as if you were playing a guitar for a packed house. It is not the time to practice scales, it's time to create and make something beautiful from the heart.

Linings

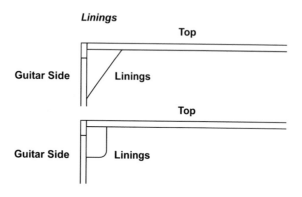

Continuing with our analogy, we'll take a closer look at the our diving board's base. This is analogous to the way the linings (sometimes referred to as kerfing in some cases) functions on the sides of the guitar. The design of the linings or kerfing of the guitar can also effect the behavior of the soundboard by limiting or encouraging spring in the perimeter area of the vibrating sound board or back.

If the base of the diving board was a square concrete block with the board itself firmly fixed to it in a way that it was solidly anchored, the base would act as an energy dam, preventing any motion at all from leaking into it. This would also be forcing the energy loaded into the board to stay in the board itself and be fully utilized. In this example, the energy comes from someone jumping on it, but in our guitar it is loaded by the motion of the bridge as we discussed in earlier chapters.

If the base of the diving board was made from a material or design that had some inherent flexibility, it would function as less of an energy dam and more of a spring. This can soften the perimeter and help to reduce some of the shrinking soundboard effect we mentioned earlier (similar to the enharmonicity of a string) due to inherent material stiffness near the edges. It also creates a situation similar to the diving board having a thinner portion near the edge which as you already know now, can encourage lower frequency behaviors.

I personally like to use un-kerfed linings, because I like to have the solid energy dam type of foundation for the perimeter of my vibrating plates—for the guitar's top and back. I then have to be sure that the thickness of my top and back (like the part of the diving board near the base) are purposefully designed and executed to achieve the desired responsiveness I need for that guitar.

Most luthiers design a guitar top—and sometimes back—that has a slightly thicker portion in the center than on the edges. This strengthens the center of the top but also helps to keep the tone of the guitar more on the warm side, allowing some of the woody tone to be present. A guitar with an even soundboard, the same thickness all the way across, will steer the tonal response and behavior of the top in a direction of encouraging higher partials of the string overtone series. And of course a guitar top with the thinnest portion in the middle will favor the higher frequencies even more than the previous examples and can sometimes become harsh and thin. These are very loose guidelines as there are so many different factors involved in the behavior and tonality of the guitar. Different types of guitars, different pieces of tone wood, and different applications call for a unique treatment to fit each situation.

Chapter 5: *Bracing*

Once the thickness and the perimeter of the soundboard have been designed to meet the requirements of the guitar that you are building, the next step is to choose a bracing pattern to suit those requirements.

Let's forget about the different types of guitars for a moment and simply look at what the bracing does for the top of the guitar. The bracing of the guitar serves a structural purpose: Not only does it keep the instrument from collapsing outright; it also helps to prevent the strings' tension from distorting the soundbox as time passes by. The bracing is also essential in defining the way the top of the guitar will vibrate. The bracing can set parameters governing the different modes of vibration of the top. Back bracing will do the same for the back, and in both cases, the bracing will have some effect on the interaction between the top and back, which is facilitated by the sides and by the soundbox's air-cavity.

1. 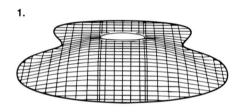 2. 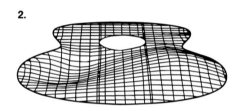 3.

Three main modes of vibration:

1. Monopole - Whole body one piece mode, in which the whole top of the guitar is moving in one piece much like a trampoline; responsible for a full sounding bass response and woofy body sound.

2. Cross dipole - Divided along the center line of the guitar with the bass and treble sides moving in opposite phase. Better treble response and near field projection.

3. Long dipole - Top divided in two, usually along the middle of the lower bought, with portions behind the bridge and in front of the bridge moving in opposite phase. One of the most important modes of vibration, because it is thought that a strong long dipole will increase projection of sound further from the instrument.

With the image in our mind of these modes, let's begin looking at the bracing of the guitar by first examining the most important brace in the entire system: the bridge. By itself, the bridge wouldn't be very efficient, but as part of the overall system it is a vital component in its own design and in how we use it to drive the soundboard and couple with the internal parts of the bracing system.

The bridge is a brace and one must learn to think of it that way. Yes, it is on the outside of the soundboard, but it is still part of the bracing structure that supports the string tension and drives the system. There are several aspects of the bridge that are critical to address in regard to the bracing system you choose, and how it is laid out within the body outline.

Bridge Position

One of the many specific topics of great importance regarding the bridge is the position of the bridge, both relative to the perimeter and shape of the guitar, and also its position relative to the internal bracing within the guitar.

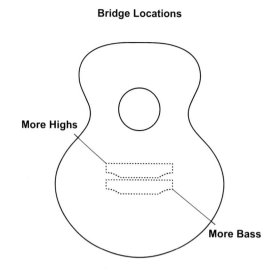

The placement of the bridge in the center of the vibrating area of the top is similar tonally to hitting a drum in the center as opposed to hitting the drum near the edge. We can use this to further engineer the type of responsiveness and tone we need into our guitar system that we are designing. I often build steel string guitars with a twelfth fret neck joint because with my design, this drops the bridge down into the center of the vibrating area of the top and gives a fuller, deeper voice. This is because as we mentioned above, we are essentially "hitting the drum in the center". The scale length we choose will also factor into the bridge position on the soundboard. A wonderfully rich voice can be obtained from a smaller body guitar with this arrangement.

Once we determine where we need to place the bridge, we can start to think about how we want the rest of the guitar to behave and respond to the string's vibrational energy. Like most everything we do to the guitar after choosing the scale length, we are almost always filtering or limiting what is happening in the system we are creating, rather than adding something new into it. The braces can limit specific behaviors or they can let that action happen more efficiently depending on how we lay them out.

A second very important concept to keep in focus regarding the bridge placement as it relates to the internal braces is that of coupling and non-coupling.

Coupling vs Non-Coupling.

A largely coupled bracing pattern will tend to move the whole guitar top as one unit. Using this gives the tone of the guitar a more woofy low-end voice. Decoupled bracing, one that is built in a way such as to let the individual braces move more independently of one another will let the top divide itself into smaller sections of vibration.

Understanding this, we can choose the appropriate overall system of bracing the guitar top, bring a greater level of control to whatever bracing we choose, and determine how strongly we want the bridge to be coupled to the tone bars inside the guitar.

I became acquainted with understanding and using the effects of bridge - tone bar coupling when I began building radially-braced guitars. The response of the guitar can be radically changed by altering the bridge-to-brace coupling. With radial bracing, each tone bar usually passes slightly under the bridge. How far we let the tone bars overlap under the bridge is our control of the amount of coupling between them. A larger overlap will make a guitar that has strong coupling from bridge-to-brace, and the guitar will have a faster response, but could be overly tight as well. A guitar with minimal overlap or coupling will have a slower response and maybe a more relaxed lyrical voice.

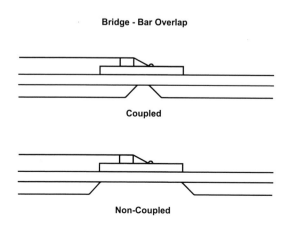

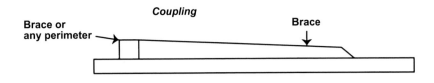

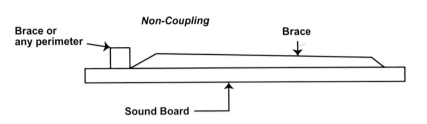

In addition to bar overlap we can also use the taper and shape of the brace to alter this relationship as it relates not only to the bridge, but also to any other brace the tone bar may approach or intersect with.

For example, with X bracing we could weaken the X intersection and then scallop the braces as they approach the sides of the guitar. This would decrease coupling and reduce (but not eliminate) the tendency of this bracing pattern to create a dominant monopole. Alternatively, we could leave all the brace ends full size and beefy. We could leave the X intersection overbuilt and even cap it with another piece of wood. This would make the coupling very strong and would limit the top's ability to flex in smaller sections. This would encourage a strong bass response (assuming that the top and tone bars are thin enough to prevent it from being non responsive due to extreme overbuilding).

One caveat; as I briefly mentioned in a previous chapter, the braces themselves limit the movement of the top and add stiffness, but they also define areas in between the braces themselves where the top could, if taken to the proper thickness, produce higher partials and frequencies. So the spaces where the bracing is NOT is important too, just something to keep in mind, as if you don't have enough to think about already.

Steel String Guitar Bracing

The most common bracing for the steel string guitar is the X bracing pattern. This pattern acts to encourage the lower top modes of vibration which is excellent for bringing some quality basses into the sound of the guitar. At the same time, the X brace design adds strength to the area in front of the bridge which is experiencing the greatest amount of downward force from the high amount of string tension present. The X brace discourages the second dipole of movement which is the plus and minus action from treble to bass sides. This helps to reduce some of the high end sound and counteract the inherently bright sounds present in the metal strings which can help bring about a better sonic balance from bass to treble frequencies.

Modes of Vibration Affected by Bracing

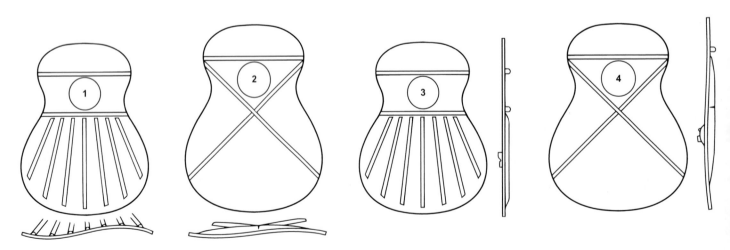

Nylon String Guitar Bracing

This pattern acts to encourage the dipole mode of vibration which is excellent for bringing some quality trebles into the sound of the guitar. On a steel string guitar this is not always wanted because there is so much treble to begin with due to the metal strings and their increased tension. But on the nylon string guitar, the makeup of the strings and their inherent sound qualities call for more focus on the trebles and less on the bass frequencies to obtain a balanced sonic envelope. The fan braces help to accomplish this balance and produce a pleasing sound through controlling the modes of vibration of the soundboard.

Archtop Guitar Bracing

The most common bracing for the archtop guitar was parallel bracing for many years. Over time it seems that the X bracing pattern has become more popular, but both styles are still used quite a bit for different applications. The way the top is behaving on the archtop guitar is different due to the different behavior of the bridge as it excites the top with vibrational energy. If you recall from earlier chapters, the archtop guitar has the strings attached to the tailpiece and as a result it is driving the top up and down like jumping on a trampoline. This sets the stage for a different type of treatment to the design of the guitar top. The soundboard is quite different from  the other guitar types that we have discussed in that it has a fairly deep arch, usually around 5/8 of an inch or so tall at the bridge location. This carved arch actually functions like a brace in a way, or at least like an extreme version of the dome that is built into many nylon and steel string guitars that we will discuss very soon in a following section. The luthier can add stiffness by then adjusting the curvature of the arch as well as the the way the thickness changes and becomes thinner as it approaches the edges of the guitar. The bracing pattern used on the archtop guitar is simplified compared to the steel string and nylon string guitars, in that there are usually only 2 braces. That being said, the top itself and its architecture is filling in the missing pieces, structurally speaking, as to how the top will interact with those 2 braces and the bridge.

On an archtop guitar, the parallel bracing pattern works in a similar manner to the fan braces on a nylon string guitar. Enabling the cross dipole mode to exist rather freely and giving the guitar a bright punchy sound with less sustain. This is great for a rhythm style guitar, and before the guitar pickup was widely used, this bracing was great for a guitarist trying to be heard with an orchestra.

These days the X brace pattern is more widely used because it unifies the top and encourages the monopole mode, giving a warmer, more sustained tone. By closing or widening the X one can control the tonality of the guitar quite a bit. A closed X pattern is more like parallel bracing giving the guitar more cutting trebles and less sustain and the wider X pattern will give the guitar more bass and a longer more complex sustain. This effect is not limited to the archtop guitar, opening and closing the X brace can also be used on the steel string guitar as well to adjust the tonality. And for that matter the fan braces on a nylon string guitar can be placed with an increased splay to grab more of the top and cut down in the cross dipole, pushing the tonality into a warmer direction as well.

Bracing Profile

Once we know the pattern or layout of the bracing pattern we will use to best control the vibrational modes of the soundboard and steer the tonality of the guitar in our desired direction, we have several more tools at our disposal to further sculpt the tone of the guitar. We can also change profile or cross section, of the braces. A taller thinner brace will enhance the clarity and high end sound. Alternatively a lower more bullet shaped brace profile will produce a warmer rounder type of sound with more bounce to it.

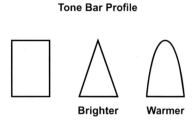

Tone Bar Profile

Brighter　　**Warmer**

You don't need to commit to one type of bracing profile or the other, though you certainly can, but you can mix and match brace profiles to get interesting effects. You might want the bass notes to have more clarity so a taller thinner more fin shaped profile could be used, and then a lower profile on the trebles. It would be more common to use the opposite of that however, with the taller thinner treble braces and the lower more rounded bass bracing profile in the area under the bass side of bridge.

Bracing Contour & Ends

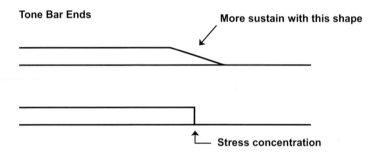

Tone Bar Ends

More sustain with this shape

Stress concentration

The side profile is another aspect of controlling the top through the shape of the braces. After experimenting with many different shapes, I have had the best results according to my tastes and those of my clients with braces that are contoured in a very organic way. In an exchange of emails with luthier Greg Buyers more than 10 years ago now, he described his braces as being shaped like bones. Luthier Eugene Clark makes his braces like the shaft of a bow, gracefully tapering toward the ends. Both of these examples stuck with me and resonated with me on an intuitive level; over the years they also proved to be very effective as I applied my own versions of these shapes to my guitars with good results.

Did you ever hear the saying, the end of something is more important than the beginning? Well that is kind of true here. The way that the brace is terminated can have a huge impact on the responsiveness of the guitar. A long taper

increases sustain, and a short, blunt, cut off will give a shorter sustain. I prefer the longer "tapered to nothing" type of brace end, because I like the sustain. Structurally speaking, I also like the fact that the stress or force from the string tension transmitted out to the ends of the brace is spread out over the long taper as opposed to the other brace termination with a sharp cut off. The latter creates a potential for stress concentration at the sharp junction between brace end and top glue joint. I am always on the lookout for stress concentration and I'm not sure if this is a real term, but I do practice a type of "stress concentration avoidance" throughout all my designs.

Top Architecture

When considering the structure of the guitar top, the luthier can choose to build a guitar with a flat top design or with a domed top design. A guitar with a flat top design is the traditional steel string guitar made by companies like Martin for many years. This type of guitar is far easier to construct and has its own type of sound that is loose and what some might describe as "traditional sounding."

The domed top has a radius of approximately 25 feet built into its geometry. This is accomplished by shaping this radius into the convex gluing surface of each brace and then gluing the braces to the top on a radiused dish having the same radius on its surface. Sometimes, flat braces can be forced into the shape of the radius by using the radius dish for gluing them. Once the braces are glued in place, the guitar top will hold its new domed shape. The 'spring fit' tension of this bracing method produces a different tonality and responsiveness from that of a flat top or a top whose braces had not been radius prior to gluing.

The original classical guitars of Torres were constructed on a dished work-board or "solera" giving the guitar top an architecture featuring a dome. This dome is part of the traditional Spanish sound. Inducing a dome into the guitar top helps to create more stiffness in the soundboard which in turn helps to counteract the pull of string tension and it does so without adding mass.

What I hear in a domed top guitar is an effect similar to tightening a drum head which makes for a more explosive response in the way the guitar reacts at the plucking of the strings. The extra stiffness also allows the soundboard to be thinned further as well, resulting again in less mass and the option to try to bring stronger trebles into the tonality of the guitar.

Chapter 6: *Tap Tuning*

The art of tap tuning seems to be confusing to many people, and I have seen it described in many different ways by different luthiers. I think it is pretty simple at its core. Everything we have talked about so far has been focusing, in one way or another, on the tuning of different aspects of the guitar's response and dimensions in order to bring them into a state of harmony. When I'm tapping the various components of the guitar, I'm looking for several different things. I'm listening to the response and decay, or the "shape" of its response over time: How it initially responds to the input, does it react quickly or slowly? Then I observe how long it sustains. I am also listening to the notes of the different components, mainly the top, back, and neck. I want them to sound pleasing together and to be close enough tonally to enable them to efficiently couple, and drive, and respond to one another when the guitar is in motion.

I don't think it is wise to spend too much time looking for specific notes because they can sometimes be misleading. If you do want to know for your records what note the top or back may be, you can sing the same note that you hear when you tap the plate. When you have matched the pitch with your voice, sing that note into your strobe tuner and see what it is or what note it is closest to.

I do this for each guitar, just to see where they land tonally. I don't try to make every guitar the same though. I aim to find harmony and make each component sound pleasing with one another. I don't have specific notes or a set formula I can give you regarding the tuning of the top, back, and air cavity of the guitar. The best advice I can offer is to start within the traditional parameters and then gradually experiment from there on a guitar-by-guitar basis. Be sure to keep detailed records of each guitar, and if possible, only make one set of changes per guitar so you will be able to accurately measure the influences of the current experiments you are conducting.

Air Cavity

Not only do we need to be sure that the top and the back of the guitar are tuned properly to achieve our goals, we also must be sure to consider the air cavity inside the guitar. This airspace is the coupling medium that ties the back and the top together. It is the medium through which the top communicates with the back of the guitar and it is responsible in part for setting the main frequency of the guitar. This main body resonance (part of the Helmholtz resonance) will be a strong component within each note of the guitar. This is especially true on guitars with back and sides made of very resonant tonewoods such as Brazilian rosewood or other members of the rosewood (Dalbergia) family. The softer woods for back and sides such as maple will have a tendency to minimize the presence of the body resonance frequency in the notes, and the more complicated sustaining overtones that would normally accompany it with rosewood.

There are two main aspects to controlling this air cavity that the builder can manipulate in order to shape the response and tone of the guitar pertaining to it.

1. The Body Depth

Increasing the body depth can bring out a fuller deeper response to bass notes and can sometimes, when taken to extremes, give the guitar a tubular sound causing a drop in mid-range frequencies. A good rule-of-thumb is that the larger the internal airspace, while maintaining the sound hole size (and all else unchanged), the lower the frequency of the body resonance.

2. The Sound Hole

The sound hole is the second component that can be used to control the resonant frequency of the internal air cavity of the guitar. Within this category of air cavity frequency controls, there are three different parameters concerning the sound hole one can use for different effects.

1. The size of the sound hole can be varied, which affects the air-cavity's Helmoltz resonance, among other things. Enlarging the sound-hole will raise the resonant frequency. That tends to give the guitar a more open and airy sound. A sound hole that is too small will produce a muted and choked and somewhat "boxy" or limited sound.

    But what is "too small?" Or for that matter, "too large?" I arrived at the sound-hole dimensions I use for each body size by assembling the body and then slowly opening the sound-hole up little by little. As I did this, I tapped and listened to the effect of each step of enlarging the hole. I did this until I arrived at a size of opening that sounded like it brought harmony to the relationship between the main top resonance and main back resonance. It is too complex to calculate, at least for me, but it is very easy if you are willing to take the time to explore it experimentally and trust your instincts to find the perfect relationship for this important aspect of your guitar design.

2. The shape of the sound hole can be varied. When the guitar vibrates, the air in the vicinity of the sound-hole can be regarded as a piston pumping in and out of the sound-hole while the air inside the guitar becomes pressurized and de-pressurized. The "piston" is usually modeled as a mass, and the enclosed air as a spring. However, different shapes of guitar sound-holes, violin and archtop f-holes, elaborately-carved "roses" on Renaissance or Baroque era instruments, and other types of openings on stringed instruments have evolved over the centuries. That tends to suggest that these openings act as more then simple masses.

    In the 1960s or 1970s, Jimmy D'Aquisto devised an analogy in which the sound-hole is likened to a garden hose. In a garden hose, the water is under pressure but flows relatively freely out of the round hole at the end of the hose. If one were to crimp the hose so that the round opening would become oval, the water would spray out of the hose to a greater distance, analogous to greater "projection" of sound.

    That analogy has stirred many debates and criticisms. But the number of different shapes of both sound-holes and f-holes tends to suggest there may well be some validity to that analogy. Moreover, none of the debates I've seen noted that every time you change the shape of the sound-hole, you are also changing the shape of the guitar's sound-board which is very important!

3. The placement of the sound hole itself can be changed. The traditional location of the sound hole on flat top guitars may or may not be the best place for the desired tonality and response you may be aiming for on your instrument. Speaking simply from a structural standpoint, the traditionally located sound-hole is directly in line with the full force of the string tension exerted by the bridge on the guitar's top. This positioning forces us to stiffen the sound hole area in order to prevent structural deformation or even collapse which can ruin the guitar's sound and playability. As you know, adding more material entails adding more mass and usually more stiffness. Unless these two attributes are introduced by choice rather than by necessity, they might detract from our ability to optimize the design of the guitar's top.

Moving the sound hole to different locations on the guitar face can have varying effects as the shape of the soundboard changes relative to the sound hole placement (and shape) and the location of the soundhole affects the internal air cavity note.

The sound-hole can even be moved off of the top entirely! Placing it in the side of the guitar can change the top's behavior more than moving it around the top can. I have experimented a lot with this specific parameter and am very satisfied with my current design which features a large sound port on the bass side of the upper bout of the guitar and no sound-hole on the face of the guitar.

Moving the sound hole off of the guitar face may seem counter intuitive at first, but if you think about it in light of what we mentioned above, it makes perfect sense. With no sound hole in the face of the guitar, one can design the tone bar / bridge system with greater freedom and more of a focus on the tonal and responsive impacts of the design, rather than being limited by the structural constraints of chopping that giant hole right in line with the string tension (which is commonly around 145lbs of force on a steel string guitar).

Side Sound-Holes & Forward Projection

Whether you have a side sound hole only, or simply add an additional sound port on your guitar, one question that many people have is this: If the sound hole is pointing up toward the player, how with the audience hear the guitar?

Well, the reason that this appears so confounding to many people is because there is a widespread misconception among many guitar players, luthiers, and music lovers which is that the sound of the guitar comes out of the sound hole of the guitar only. But in truth, a great deal of sound is radiated off of the face of the guitar as well as off of all the other components. The back and the sides and even the headstock are all producing different frequency components of the guitar's voice. Mostly the lower frequencies are coming out of the sound hole. Fortunately these lower frequencies are more omnidirectional as the frequency drops. This natural phenomenon is the reason you can place the sub woofer from your home entertainment center anyplace in the room, though the subwoofer is an extreme example since its frequencies are much lower than the guitar's lowest notes.

Higher frequency waves are much more directional and tend to stay on a somewhat linear course when they are generated. So having these higher frequencies radiating mostly off the face of the guitar makes good sense, since the face of the guitar is typically pointing at the audience.

The lower frequencies coming out of the sound hole can behave in a less linear way and sort of radiate in all directions from the source that they are generated. So having this sound hole on the side of the guitar, pointing toward the player is OK because the wave lengths coming from this source will still propagate throughout the room due to the nature of the lower frequency behavior and simply bouncing off the ceilings and walls too.

Another benefit of having the sound hole moved off of the face of the guitar is that it changes the timing of when the sound waves arrive at the ear of the listener. This sounds like a bad thing, but the result is an extremely spacial and stereo effect. The sound coming for the sound hole is likely to bounce around the room or auditorium before it reaches the ear of the listener. The high frequency signal travels in a straight line from the guitar's top to the listener. The difference is so tiny it is not perceptible consciously, but it is noticeable in a very good way. I have heard many people describe it as sounding stereo or Hi def. It really has presence and a life to it, because the space itself is factoring into the experience.

The same effect can be harnessed when recording a guitar of this design as well. One microphone can be placed near the face of the guitar, and another near the sound-hole. The audio engineer will have the freedom to pan or mix these two different signals as he or she wishes in order to produce different effects.

The Back Plate

We know that the back of the guitar is coupled to the top by the air cavity. We have also been talking about ways in which we can tune or shape the coupling and behavior of them by means of the guitar-body depth and sound hole size, shape, and placement. The back will be more responsive, or easily set in motion, if we pay special attention to its main resonant frequency (tap tone) and make sure it has the proper relationship with the guitar top's resonant frequency. This makes sense if you think about it, it's just like the feedback that you might get from an electric guitar amp when the note coming from the amp is closely related to the resonant frequency of the guitar body-cavity. We don't want the exact same thing as that feedback, but hopefully you get the idea.

With the acoustic guitar, if the top and back are closely tuned in the resonant frequency (tap tone) of each component, it is easier for one to set the other in motion and for them to communicate with one another. It is purely a matter of taste and application, but I like to have the top and back plates tuned to a maximum distance of 3 semitones. The back can be higher or lower than the top, but it should always be close enough to easily be set in motion by the top via the internal airspace compression.

Traditionally the back is braced and thicknessed to have a higher pitch than the top of the guitar. This can produce an excellent guitar as long as the distance between the pitch of the top and back isn't too much (for me its 3 semitones, for your tastes or design it might be different). A back that is tuned higher than the top will have good support for the overtones and will project very well acoustically. This is the traditional way most guitars are built for that very reason. I have personally had good results with building guitars that have a back tuned slightly lower than the top as well. These guitars have a stronger bass and work well for drop tunings and lush rich voicing. They still project very well but have a more full and deeper tone. This steers the voice into a more fundamental and pure tone which is excellent for some applications.

The most important thing is not to have a top and a back that are the same note (the same resonant frequency or tap tone). This can cause what is known as a wolf-note. These notes are the result of too much coupling at one specific frequency. The wolf-note will be louder than all the other notes, and sustain for a shorter duration than other notes. Such a note typically has a honk-like sound to it, and its effect is worst when the frequency of the resonance/s that cause it coincides with that of a note on the musical scale. The potential of encountering such a note might be lessened by being mindful of its possible relation to the position of the bridge on the top. Earlier we said that placing the bridge in the center of the top's vibrating area is similar to striking a drum at its center, and can help to obtain a deep and rich voice. But, depending on how the top's lowest mode is coupled to the back or air-cavity, placing the bridge too close to that mode's anitinode(point or region of maximum displacement when vibrating) might, figuratively speaking, awaken a sleeping wolf.

Another bit of advice is to try to keep the body cavity resonance different than the top and back as well in order to keep things in balance and even for all the notes on the fingerboard. Remember the resonant frequency of the body-cavity can be controlled by the parameters outlined in chapter 5.

Chapter 7: *Tone woods*

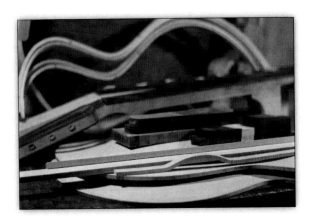

The guitar string itself, its behavior and motion has been our underlying thread that we have woven throughout our examination and discussion regarding the various components and facets of guitar design. As we begin to talk about tone-wood we will take the same approach. The wood isn't something static and dead. It is something alive and responsive, constantly reacting to input from its environment, like a guitar string. When selecting tone-wood for a guitar, we look at how the wood in question responds and processes, or colors the input that it receives, whether it is in the form of vibrational energy from a guitar string or simply from tapping on it.

We mentioned very early on in chapter 1 that once the scale length is set and the string is plucked, the input to our system we created is set. From that point on all we can do is filter or modify the existing signal. We don't have the ability to add to that signal, but rather we simply make adjustments to it and to the way we want the guitar to respond by varying the design and relationships of the different components we can control.

An equally important component to the complex, yet simple (as I hope my explanations have helped to simplify and unify the design approach rather than making it seem more complex and unapproachable) system is the tonewoods from which it is constructed. I could go into a list of each type of tone wood and the characteristics that they commonly possess, but virtually every guitar making book I have ever seen contains this information and for the most part they concur with and overlap one another. Rather than add one more set of this information into the world, let's take a different approach that I believe will be far more helpful, easy to understand, and highly applicable to your work.

Just as we did with our discussion about guitar bracing systems, let's disregard our old way of thinking and the generally agreed upon categorical thinking about tonewoods. Let's simplify the way we think about the woods we use in building our guitars all the way down to a simple set of criteria.

For example; quit thinking about the differences between woods like German spruce and Sitka spruce, because really, the string doesn't care what it is. Not only that, but the differences from one piece of wood to another vary so much that most of the common ideas about one wood species or another don't line up much of the time anyway.

I want to present you with a new way of thinking about tonewood, remember, building guitars is an art form as well as a craft. It is a science in a way, but like music, the science comes after the performance to analyze, learn from, and improve upon it. But during the performance, the art comes from the player's heart, not his mind. I approach guitar building the same way. When it's time to build and create, it's time to turn off the left brain and get in tune with your intuitive senses. Get quiet inside, still, like a pool of water. If you don't, if you're in "bull in china shop" mode and you just got done using a loud machine for hours, you will be oblivious to what the wood is subtly telling you, and where your heart is leading you.

So try picking up a piece of spruce let's say, and simply looking at it and listening to it for what it is by itself with no framework or preconceptions. Flex it, tap it, listen to the white noise generated by lightly grazing your fingers across the surface. You can even taste it, if it is sweet, it may not be old enough to use because the resins haven't hardened yet. If it tastes bland like cardboard then you know it has fully crystallized and at least in that aspect it has an advantage. Smell it, just kind of get acquainted with it, and get that kind of tactile sense based understanding that only comes from being fully present with it, you need that info to make the right decisions, many of which won't be logic based.

Mass and Stiffness

If I do look at specific characteristics of the wood, I will mostly look at the mass, the stiffness and how they relate to one another in the piece of wood. Mass in its simplest terms can be for our purposes described as the weight or even the density of the piece of wood. The weight helps us to make decisions and understand the limitations or opportunities this piece of wood has to offer us.

I think of the weight as it affects how quickly the piece can respond to energy input. It takes more energy to get a heavy object in motion than a light object. Imagine in your mind that you are pushing a tricycle. It would take very little energy to get it moving and even less to keep it moving at a consistent speed. Now imagine that you are pushing a car. Even on a flat surface, it will take a huge amount of energy get it rolling because it is so massive. Once you have it moving, it takes little energy to keep it moving at a constant speed. As a side note, a heavier object will have its own inertia, like a flywheel effect, and stay in motion longer after the driving energy input has stopped.

This behavior can be used to get the guitar to respond in the way you want it to. I typically want to make a guitar that is as lightly constructed as possible so that each note can quickly reach maximum amplitude with very little input. This helps the guitar to have a sensitivity whereby the player can lightly touch the strings and the guitar's response will be immediate and full. The density, hence weight, of the guitar's bridge is critically important in determining the response of the guitar. Adding the bridge to the center is like a weight out there, and the density of that bridge material can steer the response of the guitar drastically in one direction or another.

The weight of the wood is only half of the equation, in order for us to fully understand the potential or lack thereof, we must also know its stiffness. The stiffness-to-weight ratio is where we can begin to fully grasp what this wood is all about and how it might be used to achieve our goals as a possible component for a guitar.

There are many ways to gather this simple information. A scientific way which would involve weighing each piece and then measuring its deflection as a set amount of weight is placed on the piece. This is great for keeping records and charting the effect of various factors from guitar-to-guitar.

Personally I prefer to just listen to the wood, by tapping on it and flexing it with my hands. I used to weigh everything, but lately I have stopped because it doesn't seem necessary anymore. I feel comfortable just trusting my instincts. Maybe I needed those 15 years of cataloguing everything to help me develop enough sensitivity, like a guitar player practicing scales and exercises, over and over, year after year, until finally he can simply play and the scales have become part of him on a subconscious level, they are in his hands so to speak. I don't remember any songs anymore from my college days as a jazz guitarist, but my hands do. I can't tell you the chords, but if I just play, somehow it comes out. It's funny how that works…a little miracle.

It's the same with woods; I can tell a lot when I pick up the piece, maybe more than I could ever get by taking measurements. I don't know for sure, but I do know what seems right to me and that's the direction I strive to follow.

Chapter 8: *Visual Harmony*

Up to this point we haven't spent much time talking about the visual side of guitar design. This was intentionally done because I really wanted to illustrate the importance of designing for tone and responsiveness first and the visual aspect is second in importance. That being said, the physical proportions will affect both the visual and tonal harmony of the guitar and are of great importance.

I approach the visual aspects of guitar design no differently than any other part of the guitar. I'm looking for harmony and like the harmony we hear, the visual harmony can and should be fine tuned with the same degree of precision. Remember the guitar string, dividing into different sections corresponding to the different frequencies that made up the various overtones or partials accompanying a note? I see a version of that in objects visually. I mean, I don't consciously see it -- I get a sense of it. There is a certain moment when I know; "that's it!" Like when tuning one guitar string to another, the moment when you slightly turn the tuner knob and the beating between notes goes still and the peace of perfect unison expands like a wide open horizon in the distance.

Begin With The Tradition

As I mentioned before in preceding chapters, we as luthiers have a wonderful advantage, that of the rich history and tradition of our craft. This tradition is our starting place and foundation to help a guitar fall into the category of a "guitar" and to keep our work grounded and meaningful and in many cases help it sound good too.

When designing the body shape for example, begin with a drawing of a Martin or some other guitar you like. Then make your changes from there, little by little. Spend as much time as it takes looking at the traditional example, analyze it thoughtfully. Ask "why?", as you see the different relationships and components of the design, what is the reason for that set of choices? Keep exploring until you come to a satisfactory answer. Look for places where you see disharmonious proportions, then try some different approaches to fine tune them. All the while, keep in mind the vital importance of the way these changes will affect the sound of the guitar, which is more important than the visual aspect. The ultimate goal of course is achieving a balance between both sonic and visual optimization throughout the design.

Dimensional Harmony = Visual Harmony

Beauty might be in the eye of the beholder and there are some things that do seem to be a matter of personal preference, but I believe that under it all there is some truth, some foundational bedrock that makes us feel something is beautiful when we see it. One aspect of this that I try to incorporate into my guitar design which has been successful visually and tonally is the concept of "Visual Harmony". Another way to say it is "dimensional harmony". As my mentor Eugene Clark described it to me when he first taught it to me; "Building On the Grid".

During my studies with Eugene he demonstrated to me his findings after working on many guitars built by the Spanish masters such as Antonio De Torres and the students of Torres like Santos Hernandez. Being one of the few luthiers in modern times to work so closely with these instruments, Eugene realized after closely examining them that many of the dimensions, when measured in inches (which according to Eugene was likely to be the unit of measurement they used rather than metric measurements) are multiples of one another. Even though it is not a new idea by any means, this was a revelation to me, an epiphany to say the least.

This approach is simple, but it does require a lot of dedication and commitment to take this to the degree and level of perfection that the greats like Torress did. I spend a great deal of extra time on each guitar making sure that every component of the guitar is executed to perfection. The reason I do is because I have very intentionally chosen different measures for each component of the guitar. If I don't execute my design with precision, then the actual instrument will not reach its best potential. If for example, the headstock was designed to be 7" long and I left it at 7.020". That extra length would throw it out of harmony. You wouldn't want to play a guitar where the strings were just tuned "close enough," would you? Looking at something that is almost in tune gives me a similar feeling.

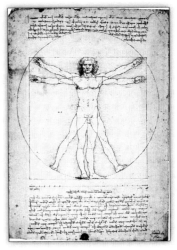

It works like this, I first choose a master dimension. I like to use .025" because it is the unifying measurement between 10ths and 8ths of an inch. This fact is very important as you will see. I might use this as the width of my purfling lines or some other small detail of the design.

Then the next step is to make sure that every other component on the guitar is divisible by that number. This ensures that each component is literally harmonized dimensionally with one another.

Using .025" gives you the ability to use 8 ths for one part and then 10 ths for another and still having them both divisible by your master dimension.

This might seem a little extreme, and I'll admit it is! But I feel that I can see and hear the difference. I'm not after average or good when it comes to my work, and I have a strong feeling that if you are reading this book right now you aren't satisfied with it either. WE are striving for exceptional and truly remarkable! I take any means necessary to try to create a "musical instrument", one that breathes and has that "voice" and life to it that we have discussed so much in this text.

Great Art Tells A Story

One of the differences between the paint on a wall and a painting that is hanging on the wall is the story that the latter tells, the feeling that it conveys, that is what makes it "Art". I like to think of my guitars as a piece of art that tells its unique story. A very subtle one that maybe no one could unravel, but never the less it's there woven into the very dimensions of every part infusing and uniting all the different components into something more, into a work of art.

There is a story that is meaningful to me personally that I use quite a bit and one way to incorporate it into my work is to build my design around the numbers 7 and also 26. I will let you try to decipher this story for yourselves if you ever get the chance to see one of my guitars in person, but even if one doesn't understand it literally, there is still something there, something more than just another object. To me that is very important.

I won't get into much detail here because it is up to you to find your way to tell your story, but to illustrate this concept here is an example; I might build a fan fret guitar around the number 7. I could make the 7th fret the master fret (the one that the two scales emanate from), then I could make the headstock 7" long. I could make the difference of the scales .7", I could make the body 14" wide, and so on weaving this theme into every part and remember this is all happening on top of the framework we talked about before (the grid) where every component is a multiple of the master dimension I chose.

When I am thinking of my guitar from a design perspective, in my mind it looks like a wire-frame of numbers and points of light—a constellation.

And like a constellation the position of each point represents something, I'm not drawing a picture literally, but I am alluding to different things with my placement and subtle choices of my measurements for each part and how they relate to one another.

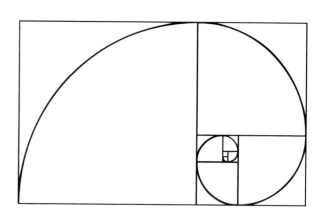

There is a very specific order to what I'm doing, I mean an organization or a harmonization. Like in nature and like the stars and the planets and how they work together and interact and even work together mathematically, with this same type of dimensional harmony and harmonious behaviors and relationships. I am in no way saying it must be done this way, I'm just saying this is the way I feel led to create my guitars, my contribution…my art.

Chapter 9: *Finishing*

The finish of the guitar is the final piece of the puzzle, and a very important one at that. The finish not only protects the wood, but it is the link between the wood and the air around it as well as a potentially limiting hard shell covering the surface. In the early years of my career I sprayed nitrocellulose lacquer on my guitars. It's a good finish, flexible enough to last and move with the wood and somewhat durable too, enough to handle day to day abuse. But it does have some serious drawbacks too. It is flammable and even though you have read this before please take note this time, it is VERY flammable. Even the overspray after being dry for years is like gasoline. I learned this the hard way. I almost lost my home and shop because a spark ignited some very light overspray on the wall where my exhaust fan used to be. Within a moment, everything was in flames. Thankfully I had a fire extinguisher nearby and was able to put it out. I'm telling you this to warn you because it is easy to underestimate the danger of the chemicals both in flammability and toxicity.

One of my mentors, luthier Eugene Clark once told me this: "The rules of safety are written in the blood of injured men" he is right, follow the rules…be careful.

My Story

I was miserable in my toxic and dangerous Nitrocellulose mess, but I felt it was the best for my guitars and I was willing to do whatever it took to make my work the best it could be, even possibly shortening my own life (pretty dumb in retrospect).

Then one day, I had just finished a nylon string guitar and was packing it up to ship it to its new home. As I was closing the case for the last time, the light caught some flaws in the finish. I didn't see it before that moment and I decided that I couldn't live with it. Spraying more lacquer would possibly repeat the same issue I was seeing, so I decided to strip the top and French polish it instead.

Before I noticed the flaws, the guitar was totally finished, and I had spent hours playing it and getting to know its tone and responsiveness and was very pleased with it. What I didn't realize is that my understanding of guitar finish was about to be totally and radically changed forever. I stripped the top and over the next several weeks, I applied a glossy and beautiful french polish finish to it. I restrung the guitar, and I will never forget the moment I played the newly French polished guitar for the first time. It was astonishing! It didn't just sound a little bit better, it was 100 times better! It was so open and full of vibrancy and life. It was the same guitar, but with more breath, and more life flowing through its voice. Even the way it felt as I held it was different somehow, less like dead weight, more like something alive than it was before.

I had often noticed that when I would take a guitar back out of the spray room after being sprayed with Nitro it would seem heavier, like it took on some dead weight. When I French polish a guitar, I get a sense that the guitar becomes lighter and more alive than with no finish at all.

The choice of what type of finish to use on your guitars will be a very personal one that only you can make. Keep in mind though, what goals you want to achieve with your guitars and, most importantly, be honest with yourself. Be honest with what you are actually putting as the first priority, and be honest with your assessment of your work. Find a good comparison to help give your work some perspective against which to make judgments.

If you decide that using a specific type of finish to go faster and be more profitable is the first priority then that is OK. Most guitar makers that are making good money are doing this. But if you really and truly want the best sound possible (which every luthier claims) then you might want to at least try the experiment I described above. Spray the guitar with the faster synthetic finish, then play it. Strip it, French polish it and play it again. Only then will you know the truth of how the finish is affecting your guitar. Comparing two different guitars is helpful, but not nearly as beneficial as doing the experiment on the same guitar.

Chapter 10: *Final Thoughts*

A Reminder

Before you get too overwhelmed and lost in the scientific world of modes and structural engineering, let me remind you once more that your ear and your intuition should be your primary guide. Play as many guitars as you can with different bracing patterns as you can. Listen closely and honestly. Find the sound you like, and use the system producing that sound as a starting point for your experimentation.

When I began building guitars, I benefited from the advantage of having played guitars for many years. I was a jazz guitar major earning my bachelors of music degree with a double major in Jazz Guitar and Audio Technology which entailed playing guitar for many hours every day. All that time deeply listening and getting to intuitively know the guitar and its intricate and unique qualities formed the basis of my personal tastes and understanding of how the guitar responds for the perspective of the player first. I began building guitars after completing my degree, having acquired the ear and sensibilities of a player rather than those of a woodworker.

I mention this because it is so critical to stay focused on the player and the fact that you are creating a musical instrument. An instrument is completely different from just about any other object I can think of. Don't ever start viewing the guitar as just a box or it will become just that.

Goals

In order to achieve success with any design the first step is to define the goals of that specific guitar. I strongly recommend writing out these goals in order to solidify them and cause you to wholeheartedly commit to them throughout the entire process and every step of your design and building phases. Without a clear and defined goal you will be wandering around aimlessly in your efforts, and the guitar in the end will lack focus from a design standpoint, and be a reflection of your attitude and approach during its creation.

In order to master the craft of guitar making or any craft for that matter, one must learn to make every movement and every decision with great intent and decisive determination. No motion, not even a single strike of sandpaper across the wood, should ever be randomly or pointlessly carried out. Throughout every step, your mind and the vision in your mind's eye must be clearly focused on the end result. If you don't the guitar will suffer, and you ultimately end up with mistakes, oversights, and a building experience that is much less mastery.

Glue Joints

Understanding your different glues and anticipating the effect inside your glue joint is critical for a master level guitar. I almost never make two flat surfaces to glue together. I am always thinking on a microscopic level as to what will be happening inside the glue joint. Some joints need tension or spring inside them; others need to be at rest. Never just slap two flat pieces together because they may not be flat after the glue is introduced. A flat surface that gets water based glue like Tightbond or hot hide glue on it will immediately spring outward and leave you with two surfaces that are open all around the edges from the water expanding the wood cells and making the wood warp a tiny bit. These tiny microscopic bits make a big difference as they are summed up into the final guitar.

Make a musical glue joint. Try this experiment; make one glue joint with 2 perfectly flat surfaces, and another with the gluing surfaces slightly (just a couple thousandths) concave, and glue your blocks together. When dry, drop each one on a steel table, if you have done it right, you should hear a better sound from the one that you anticipated effects of water based glue on the wood. The other will sound more like two pieces of wood and have less ring to it. The block in which the glue joint was compensated for the effect of the glue will certainly look better with a tighter and stronger seam.

Apply this type of detail oriented thinking and precision execution to your guitar, and you may have an instant improvement!

Don't put the cart before the horse

A beautiful guitar will never be enough unless it sounds beautiful too. Way too many builders make the mistake of focusing their efforts on creating a guitar that looks great, but sounds…OK. From a business model perspective it seems to make sense, because people do often buy with their eyes and not their ears. In other words, they buy the one with the most "bells and whistles" and that looks the best or has the most familiar brand name. But the problem with this approach is that in time, just being beautiful or a popular brand won't be enough. There has to be a voice in the guitar, a beautiful sound and responsiveness that will call to the player year after year and inspire him with fresh passion and insight every time he picks it up. Without this magic, this true voice, the guitar, even though it might look good, becomes just another pretty thing and eventually will get sold or at best sit collecting dust year after year.

If you want to be a true artist you have to understand this truth and apply it to your craft. Focus your efforts first on finding your sound, your voice. Yes, make it look good, but always keep your priorities in line. The voice is the heart and soul of the guitar, it is the spark that makes what we do as luthiers special, that gives it life, and breath, and excites, and inspires.

Tom Bills Guitars

Natura Deluxe 17" Archtop

About The Author

On March 21 1992 an unsuspecting 16 year old kid named Tom Bills walked into a staff lodge at a weekend camp where he had been helping a friend for the weekend. He heard a sound as he approached the door and it instantly began to resonate within him in a way that was undeniably important.

Upon entering the room Tom realized it was the sound of an acoustic guitar. I am not sure how he managed to go 16 years without seeing a guitar in person before, but somehow it just made this fateful moment that much more awe inspiring. Captivated and smitten with the instrument, he watched and listened in awe. The song was, "Wish You Were Here", by Pink Floyd. Two other camp counselors where playing together, one on a twelve string, and the other on a six string.

By the end of that evening Tom had already learned to play two songs. Less than a week later on March 26th for his 17th birthday Tom got his first acoustic guitar. By the start of the next school year Tom tried out for the high school jazz band and beat out several other students to get the spot. It was there that his love for jazz deepened and grew, as well as his passion for the guitar.

Tom didn't come from a very musical family, his grandfathers, and even great grandfathers were all craftsmen and wood workers. Casmiro Polizzi , Tom's great grandfather was an incredibly skilled metal and wood worker, who after coming to America from Polarimo, Sicily, spent most of his working life as an inventor for the Cadillac Co. His grandfather Russell Bills was a small engine mechanic and cabinet maker. Tom's other grandfather John Polizzi was a skilled carpenter back in the days before power tools. Tom's father, Tom Bills senior, followed the family tradition and became a talented carpenter as well.

Many of the tools in Tom's workshop were handed down to him from his father and grandfathers, adding an extra element of history to the work space and a tangible aspect to the skills that these men also passed on to Tom.

While earning his Bachelors of Music degree with a double major in Jazz Studies and Audio Technology, Tom was able to study under the legendary audio engineer, Bill Porter, who was well known for his recordings of Roy Orbison, Elvis, and many others. Bill Porter had an impact on the way Tom listened to a room and thought about sound. Since Porter came from an era of audio engineering before the modern digital age, his techniques relied heavily on the ability to acutely listen to, and analyze the sound of a musical instrument.

Tom completed his first guitar during his junior year and brought it to his daily classes and guitar lessons with some of the top guitar players in St. Louis at the time. His instructors quickly noticed the striking quality in Tom's first guitar and some even commissioned Tom to build guitars for them.

Shortly after graduation, tragedy struck. While doing a weekend home improvement project, Tom's right hand was severely broken. Spiral fractures in the metacarpals that were, according to doctors, impossible to set properly. The doctors told Tom that he would never have full use of his right hand again.

In a literally miraculous series of events Tom's hand was fully healed with no scar tissue or limitations of mobility whatsoever. Around this time Guitar Center opened its first store in St Louis, which happened to be near where Tom lived. Upon the urging of family members, Tom reluctantly took his first guitar there to see if they might be interested in buying some to sell in their stores. To his utter shock, they were so impressed, they ordered 3 guitars on the spot. Tom recalls that day; " up until then, I knew that I loved making guitars and that it was something I could just do naturally, but I think it finally sunk in because of the way everyone kept reacting to my guitars, and that day, Tom Bills Custom Guitars was officially born. "

Tom has gone on to gain international recognition by guitar players and collectors as one of the top luthiers living today and continues to refine his art, handcrafting some of the most sought after and unique guitars in the world.

 **THEARTOFLUTHERIE.COM**

 https://www.facebook.com/TheArtOfLutherie
https://www.facebook.com/TomBillsCustomGuitars

 https://twitter.com/artoflutherie
https://twitter.com/tombillsguitars

Additional resources, tutorials, luthier classes, and more can be found at:

TheArtofLutherie.com
TBguitars.com

Credits

Photos:	Tom Bills and Matt Bills
Video/DVD:	Matt Bills
Editing:	Gila Eban
Graphic Design:	Charlie Lee-Georgescu

Notes

Notes